THE SCIENCE BEHIND

BATMAN'S

FLYING MACHINES

by
Tammy Enz

BATMAN created by
Bob Kane with Bill Finger

SCIENCE BEHIND
BATMAN

Curious Fox
...mpany-publishers for children

Published by Curious Fox, an imprint of Capstone Global Library Limited, 7 Pilgrim Street, London, EC4V 6LB
—Registered company number: 6695582

www.curious-fox.com

STAR37308

ISBN 978 1 78202 543 6
20 19 18 17 16
10 9 8 7 6 5 4 3 2 1

A CIP catalogue for this book is available from the British Library.

Editorial Credits
Christopher Harbo, editor; Hilary Wacholz, designer; Wanda Winch, media researcher;
Tori Abraham, production specialist

Artwork by Luciano Vecchio and Ethen Beavers

Photo Credits
Library of Congress: Prints and Photographs Division, 7; NASA: Artwork by Steve Lighthill, 9; Shutterstock: Chris Parypa Photography, 8, MO_SES_Premium, 6; U.S. Air Force, 15 (left), Staff Sgt. Bennie J. Davis III, 21, Staff Sgt. Brian Ferguson, 17; U.S. Marine Corps photo by Cpl. Garry J. Welch, 14; U.S. Navy photo, 13, Mass Communications Specialist 2nd Class Brian Morales, 12, Mass Communications Specialist Seaman Timothy A. Hazel, 18, MC3 Mark El-Rayes, 11 (top), Photographer's Mate 3rd Class Joshua Karsten, 19; Wikimedia: Bernd. Brincken, 11 (bottom)

Printed in China.

CONTENTS

INTRODUCTION

SUPER HERO WINGS

The Caped Crusader commands the skies. With his Batplane and Batcopter, Batman tracks down super-villains in the most challenging places. From **supersonic** flight to **vertical** take-offs, his flying machines are packed with amazing features. Best of all, many real aircraft have these features too.

supersonic faster than the speed of sound
vertical straight up and down

CHAPTER 1
FLIGHT PERFORMANCE

The Batplane uses the same science as real aircraft. Aeroplane wings are round at the front and **tapered** at the back. Their shape allows air to flow faster over the top than underneath. This air movement creates **lift** to push planes skywards.

In the 1890s, German engineer Otto Lilienthal built gliders inspired by the shape of bird wings.

taper become narrower at one end

lift upward force of air that causes an object to fly

The Dark Knight uses the Batplane's powerful jets to chase down criminals. Real jet engines burn fuel to release rapidly expanding gases. These gases then create **thrust** to push planes forwards. Some jet engines provide enough thrust to fly faster than the speed of sound.

An F-18 Super Hornet creates a vapour cone as it breaks the speed of sound.

NASA's X-43A holds the record as the world's fastest aircraft. It reached a speed of nearly 11,265 kilometres (7,000 miles) per hour.

thrust force that pushes a vehicle forwards

To fly in tight areas, Batman uses the Batcopter's **rotor** power.

rotor set of rotating blades that lifts an aircraft off the ground

Most helicopters in our world have two sets of rotors. The main rotor on top creates lift. The smaller rotor on a helicopter's tail provides balance. Without balance a helicopter would spin out of control.

Spinning rotors allow an MH-60 Seahawk helicopter to hover above a ship's deck.

FACT

The Eurocopter X3 has two small rotors on its sides instead of its tail. These rotors make it more stable and faster than most helicopters.

CHAPTER 2
AMAZING ABILITIES

The Batplane takes off and lands on the shortest of runways. Some real fighter jets take off and land on very short aircraft carrier runways. A **catapult** helps fling jets off the ship for quick take-offs. The jets use tail hooks to catch a cable for short landings.

An F-16 Super Hornet catches a cable to land on an aircraft carrier.

The US Navy catapulted its very first aircraft off the USS *North Carolina* on 5 November 1915.

catapult device used to launch areoplanes from the deck of a ship

What if there's no runway at all? That's no problem for the Batplane. It can take off and land like a Harrier Jump Jet. This fighter plane's jets fire downward for vertical take-offs and landings. Once in the air, the pilot changes the angle of the jets for normal flight.

A night-vision camera captures the vertical thrust of the Harrier Jump Jet.

FACT

In the 1950s, the Ryan X-13 Vertijet was designed to launch from a submarine. It could take off and land on its tail.

Batman's aircraft sometimes fly without a pilot at all. The US military has more than 10,000 unmanned aircraft. One of them is the MQ-9 Reaper combat drone. It can lock on to moving targets from 15,240 metres (50,000 feet) above Earth.

An MQ-9 Reaper drone comes in for a landing.

CHAPTER 3
ENGAGING ENEMIES

A sailor checks a Sidewinder heat-seeking missile.

Batman's flying machines use **precise** missiles to disarm enemy aircraft. Many military fighter jets carry heat-seeking missiles. These missiles lock on to the heat produced by enemy aircraft. The Sidewinder heat-seeking missile can fly 16 kilometres (10 miles) to reach its target.

smart bomb

Guided missiles and bombs are called
"smart bombs". They are programmed or
steered to destroy specific enemy targets.

precise very accurate or exact

Batman's aircraft use **stealth** mode to catch villains off guard.

stealth ability to move secretly

radar device that uses radio waves to track the location of objects

The B-2 Spirit bomber also flies with stealth. Its flat shape and sharp angles make it invisible to enemy **radar**. Its engines also have noise shields. The B-2 can fly close to enemies without being heard.

B-2 Spirit bomber

Batman's aircraft command the skies with state-of-the-art features. The real world science behind them is as amazing as the Caped Crusader himself.

GLOSSARY

catapult device used to launch aeroplanes from the deck of a ship

lift upward force of air that causes an object to fly

precise very accurate or exact

radar device that uses radio waves to track the location of objects

rotor set of rotating blades that lifts an aircraft off the ground

stealth ability to move secretly

supersonic faster than the speed of sound

taper become narrower at one end

thrust force that pushes a vehicle forwards

vertical straight up and down

READ MORE

The Big Noisy Book of Planes, DK (Dorling Kindersley, 2016)

Diary of a Pilot (Diary of a...), Angela Royston (Raintree, 2014)

Great Aircraft Designs (Iconic Designs), Richard Spilsbury (Raintree, 2015)

Helicopters, Emily Bone (Usborne Publishing, 2011)

How to Draw Batman and His Friends and Foes (Drawing DC Super Heroes), Aaron Sautter (Raintree, 2015)

INDEX

READ THEM ALL!

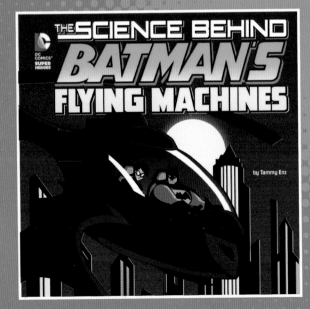

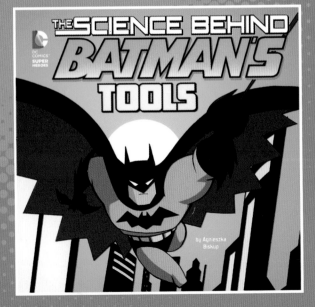